Sam Smith
the complete pieces

Newton-le-Willows

Reviews of *The Pieces*

' ... This powerful book is well worth the money not only for its unassuming psychological insights but for the exquisite sensual images that pervade, all of which are startlingly English. Don't be deterred by the subject matter, this is not a squeamish book; it is a book that explores our values of life and it is a book about endurance and beauty. About 60 pages long, its unshrinking, forthright style make it quite quick to read (I didn't want to put it down) but the images therein linger long after the turning of each page. Pieces should not be left sitting on any publisher's shelf; it should be dog-eared and passed on.'
– **Carol Thistlethwaite:** *Tregolwyn Book Reviews*

Rip Bulkeley said - of some of those already published, in this case in the River King Poetry Supplement (USA) - ' ... suddenly I ran into something not just good but great, a poem which I hope has already gone round the world but if not should do so as soon as possible. It is Sam Smith's PIECES, an exhibition of 21st-century war via the small-town concentration camp ... '
– *NHI Online Review*

' ... a captivating exploration of love, grief, and especially hope in a prisoner of war camp ... But Pieces is also about violence, and therein lies something fascinating and even beautiful ... The lines are musical, lulling ... creates an enchanted, awful place where people are dying, where we don't want them to stop dying, so we can keep reading ... '
– **Donna Biffar:** *Orbis #121*

' ... one of the best books to have appeared in [the] UK so far this century ... '
    – **Jeremy Hilton:** *Fire #19*

' ... The descriptive density and personal revelation of the experience give these 'pieces' poetic weight ... Smith has a winning style ... '
    – *The Black Mountain Review #6*

' ... Smith's language has an abstract and untethered feel, but his descriptions of the natural cycle of life continuing beyond and without reference to the prisoners are compellingly precise ... '
    – **L. Kiew:** *NHI Online Review*

' ... prose-poetry items which stand alone, or as a landscape of observations ... This is a new approach; you need to read it yourself.'
    – **Geoff Stevens:** *Purple Patch #101*

Published in the United Kingdom in 2024
by The Knives Forks And Spoons Press,
51 Pipit Avenue,
Newton-le-Willows,
Merseyside,
WA12 9RG.

ISBN 978-1-916590-03-8

Copyright © Sam Smith 2024.

The right of Sam Smith to be identified as the author of this work has been asserted by them in accordance with the Copyrights, Designs and Patents Act of 1988. All rights reserved. No part of this publication may be reproduced, stored in a retrieval system, transmitted in any form or by any means, electronic, photocopying, recording or otherwise, without prior permission of the publisher.

Acknowledgments:

Some of these poems have been published in groups and singly in *Borderlines, Braquemard, Cadenza, Envoi, Konfluence, Moonstone, Obsessed With Pipework, Poetry Monthly, River King Poetry Supplement, Sepia, South* and the *'Wow!'* jazz anthology.

My thanks especially to Kevin Troop (K. T. Publications, 16 Fane Close, Stamford, Lincolnshire, PE9 1HG, UK) who in 2001 published, as part of his 'Kite modern poetry series' a paperback, mail order only, version of 'pieces'.

the complete pieces

Love is love: a tenderness shown, fingertips
brushing at specks on a beloved's shoulder;
unconscious acts of familiarity, hand or wrist
taken when walking, and the whole body turning
in towards and touching the other, hip to chest. Love.

> Tower guards fire bursts down at the dogs
> that disturb the graves beyond the fence.
> Gate sentries have been seen to follow,
> with their gunsights, a highflying crow
> or gull, say "Bang." The dogs are left unburied,
> grave rags and pink bones partially uncovered.

Bartering morsels for medicines, attentive to
the other's every breath, this one man advertises
his love, beams his pleasure in his lover's recovery.
Other prisoners look on this enactment of love's gestures
with dumb wonder, recall themselves being fathers,
that same gentling kiss upon a son's sharp hair,
headslant smile of companionship to a beside-them wife.

Sam Smith

A slow drizzle collects on latitudes of wire.
Drops congregate, meet and merge, run along
to the lowest point, and drip; shattering on lower
strands and making miniature cascades. Singular
drops snail backwards down the vertical.

> Believing all water here, because it is here,
> to be undrinkable, dehydration has created a
> vitamin B deficiency, adding to his delusional
> state. The already lack of vitamin C
> means that his skin has spots and lesions,
> his gums are swollen and his teeth loose.

Beyond the rhomboids, ellipses and rectangles of the fence
are waist-sawn stumps and lime-spattered graves. Beyond these
sunken and hummocked oblongs is a line of sparkling trees
– a few birch beckoning lightness; but mostly the inner dark
of conifer. Beyond the trees' wispy tips a mountain, its peak
wearing a cyclist's helmet of cloud. From the diamond-mesh
gate, the road curves into the green-black trees.

The human brain weighs just over a kilo, has
ten billion nerve cells. Physical sensation of a new
idea is that of a curtain thrown back, or of two
matrixes connecting, eyes coming wide with
comprehension ... most idiots are occasionally savant.

> On the guardhouse birdtable, it's the male sparrow
> who anxiously tends the fledgling, grown in all
> but tail, that flutters and wide-beaked cheeps
> at him. Soon as the parent flies out through the
> fence, the young bird unfluffs its insistent
> helpless pretense, pecks with smooth efficiency.

Rainbellied clouds hang over the towers. A young
man, sense of self gone, breaks off a piece
of plastic guttering and, weeping his despair,
swings it and pokes it at other prisoners.
A guard, in passing, shoots him, comes to examine
the body, his face cheerfully expecting the attacked
men to be grateful. He studies their grief.

Sam Smith

He wears the secret smile of an unassailable man.
Certain of his own death, nothing bad can be done
to him again. Springtime birds are frantically feeding.
He leaves a clip of scrawled poems dedicated to his
'always dead self', and woven with an intricate symbolism.

> Tower guards, irked by their apparent
> complacent waddling, shoot to kill at
> the crows; but only to scare, chuckling,
> the dogs away from the graves. Because
> they, once, petted dogs like those? Crows,
> caught young, it is argued, can be tamed too.

The hut's 'would-be scholars' disagree over
the poems' meanings. One says, getting louder
(and hope is as essential as food here): "suicide
is no sanctification of any truth, is simply
an obsession fulfilled or a life found to be
not worth living." White florets on leafless
blackthorn speckle the background of conifers.

Where death and dispossession are arbitrary,
where life is only as certain as the last meal
(not the next), the unusual is frightening. But
food will be taken from the dead man's bowl;
and his clothes, if not whole, used as patches.

> Out of this day's wormbright sky, the mountain's
> grey peak has attracted a single white cloud;
> which, having been caught, has to slide and
> slither free. The ring of dark firs have new green
> branch ends, brown candle stamens. In a naked
> blackthorn is a winter-collapsed magpie's nest.

When death is daily anticipated, but unpredictable
– the guard does not, at that moment, like the look
of you; or has decided beforehand (to prove to
himself or to others) to shoot the nineteenth
prisoner he sees that day, and the one standing
to the left of him – then a man can come up with no
schemata for survival, build no value system from it.

Sam Smith

The guards wear white convex masks and genuflect
as the blue-skinned cadavers are carried out to
the fires. (Rumour is the disease is an experiment,
prisoners expendable.) An orange sun and a white moon
take turns to float in the weaving of black smoke.

> (Rumour is the guards have been secretly
> vaccinated.) More prisoners, feet bleeding,
> are pushed in through the gates. Their camp
> was bulldozed. (Rumours are of more killing,
> of guards needed elsewhere, of a war lost,
> a war won, of more prisoners taken.)

The tower guards only pretend to shoot at the rooks that
daily arrange themselves in the died-back branches
of an oak. (Rumour is of a village or town in that direction.)
Daylong grind of heavy machines has rumour of tanks, then
of a convoy. Final conclusion is combine harvesters,
a dust haze silting the sky to the east. One guard one day
is merciful over a dropped bowl. (Rumour is of release.)

A cirrus sky-frost re-patterns the sky,
creates a double smear of westering sun –
replicating itself in a herringbone
segment of refracted rainbow. Up,
up there, a planing gull cries, and cries.

> The white man in the shower, beaten blue
> face down among pink suds, and crouched
> in a fearful death; backside dripped upon;
> has an arsehole like a purple mouth. Thin
> slippery limbs straightened – for carrying –
> the anus becomes a brown asterisk.

A meadow brown butterfly, on day's warmed
stone, opens its wings, a one-page book.
When flown, the kneeling man looks over to
the guardhouse garden, watches petals close
around day's end sun, considers
properties of colour and light, the electro-
chemical processes of thought and being.

Sam Smith

A passing through shower divides
the camp into light-dry/dark-wet
as arbitrary as life/death. A quiet
guard says, "All I'm doing here
is my job." He can take a tablet.

> Plasmodium is a protozoan causing
> malaria. Vector is the mosquito.
> The infected are not infectious to men,
> only, once parasites develop, to a new
> biting mosquito, sucking in pathogens.
> Here men walk the geography of the head,

an idea of roads, explore the inner universes
of cranial folds, with each their childhood cast
in neural perspex, a static time and place,
ageless each for each its owner's lifespan. Parts
may be temporarily hidden by memory's mirrors,
revealed upon re-examination. None, though,
characters nor landmarks, can be changed.

Summer green, this showery day – each tree
picked out in 3D rain-bright clarity;
part-moon the same dirty white as
the wisp-ends of clouds, fledglings foolish
funny in their false starts and alarms.

> Longer they too are caged the more the guards
> regress. In idleness they draw on and dye their
> arms and chests, add ribbons to their caps, plait
> leather and metal round their wrists. One has
> come by a short spear, another a sword. Soon he
> will invent a ritual for the chopping off of heads.

Clouds have lain hold of the mountain. Two
jackdaws, in a glide, fall across the sky.
In the lee of an oak a squad of rooks surf
the eddies, sliding up over one another,
skimming down the wind's face. Gusts push
and pull at a trailing bramble, which saws
and shreds a hazel's wide leaves, winning light.

Sam Smith

A half-dead plant, feeding on its own decay, produces
a single blue, bell-like bloom beside a floor support.
To each man's surprise other prisoners reveal themselves
to be aesthetes too; and, in corners, they marvel together
at the sheer magnitude of each their own life's being.

> For three days, beside the parched tamped earth
> of the compound, this one white-starred flower,
> its broken stem leaking jewels of sap, becomes
> an object of reverence. In clear sight of a tower,
> however, these pilgrims do not kneel: they hang
> a step, join in praise where not overlooked.

With the nose-wrinkle of a glasses-wearer he looks up
to skylark and swallow singing on the wing, points out
the black round eye of a magpie, blue of a daw, the fat
semi-discs of bracket fungus shelving a birch; and, on
a concrete post, elfin pillows of brittle lichen. The commonplace of beauty is agreed upon. The shock, always with men,
for men, is how quick and absolute is death.

When death and dispossession are arbitrary
superstitions can crowd a life – touch wood,
shuffle and barge for your lucky number place
in the queue, count crows, wish on rainbows ...
today's bullet will not go in the back of your head.

> Dollops of rounded cloud float,
> bottoms flattened, on an air surface
> unseen. Between huts thin men edge
> through a golden insect soup, aspergic
> hands flicking and counting, or making
> gestures, as if in excited conversation.

A bellow of authority's exasperation, definition
of a single shot, crow bark of an order, galloping
thud of two men in a stumbling run. Spectacles
a step away, the body has fallen at a twist,
attracts each man with each his sneer of
fascination. The face, minus its glasses,
nose indented, looks naked and cross-eyed.

Sam Smith

Among fence weeds, below the louder flower-
rattle of wing buzz, with exo-skeletal
vibrations, insects are talking one to another.
A poison-killed mole has its poignant
pink hands spread upon its velvet chest.

> This day of white cloud and showers has
> a clear blue light squeezed between sky and
> land. In this strange normality – new-mown
> smell of grass-sap – an old man with a
> coxcomb of grey hair, is dragging his age
> and his illness around with him.

Sparrows hop and drop from the low shrub hedge
around the guardhouse garden. Longtailed tits fall
slantwise, like flakes of light, from fir branch to
dark fir branch. In among this screen of trees one grey
pigeon steps sideways along a branch. A songthrush
runs beakdown across the guardhouse lawn, pronged
comes to a halt. The pigeon cracks into flight.

Under a wierding sky, cloud underbelly
of yellow, three fast pigeons veer apart
over the camp. A falcon, in a featherburst,
takes the centre pigeon, drops to ground
beyond the trees. To be part of the event

> men, breathing again, move silently towards
> the falling feathers, catch one or stoop
> to the compound, hold it in their pocket.
> Such men need, always, to belong – to a tribe,
> and to know their status within that status.
> Here the guards impose categories too;

but nothing fits. It is the most brutal of
the guards who acts as middleman in barter
with the outside farmers; meeting the prisoners
at day's end, where a few men gather to watch
the mountain peak – above and beyond the masking
trees, and squared off by the fence – turn
an inky blue: to be a part of the moment.

Sam Smith

The wind is visible only in its effect:
gale-snatched leaves get slapped against
hut sides, wind-blown birds are dark
streaks past windows, rain-blacked
tree trunks are falsely shadowed.

> Stories, stale to their tellers, tell of
> lives before; but so strange, so different
> to now are these tales that even the tellers
> don't believe them. Such histories do,
> however, serve to give men names – Teacher,
> Carpenter, Farmer, Tailor, Fishman, Brickie ...

Most men here, prisoners and guards, one
or the other, are so alike they could have
stepped out of each other's mouths. A stranger,
though, can't know how many miles a man's
got in his boots, the pace they've been at,
terrains they've known. Afraid, most men
will hide behind a moustache, or a scowl.

Made passive spectators of their own
lives, men watch themselves obey. Ragged
rooks flop over tree tops. Jays squawk
over acorns. None here any longer
question the bizarre as normal.

> Across broken glass a spider has
> built a web. With his fingertip he
> marvels at both how strong and how
> sticky each strand is, yet how easily
> broken. Returns to old thoughts,
> scratches at bites already bitten.

Nine prisoners are tied wrist to wrist.
The guard, pistol casually held, shoots
those men on either end first, works
his way implacably in towards the man
in the middle. He, anchored, screaming,
tugs bodies this way, that, frantic
as a spider in a hailstorm.

Sam Smith

Wind-blown plastic has snagged
branches, got wrapped around
knobbled twig-ends, been shredded
by gales, ribboned; has made of this
still-standing oak a fetish tree.

> No life here, states rather
> measured in degrees of
> degradation. Confined, men grow
> twisting around one another,
> reaching each for their truth,
> singleminded on survival.

Fawn clouds have trapped
below them an amber light:
either a haze of common fart dust
or pollen from an angel's wings.
Whichever ... pressing themselves
back against hut walls, eyes part
closed, men try not to breathe.

Whosoever's the single death, whosoever
grieves, the intricacies of life go on.
Small white globes, strung along
the treeless soil, are stunted tentacles
of a filament mass of fungus underground.

> The great tit, hanging off the birdtable,
> wears his sergeant's stripes upon his back.
> Across the guardhouse lawn robin and
> thrush two-legged hop. Stop. Listen.
> Hop. The guard's hawk-sharp face
> is at odds with his big soft bum.

Puddle reflection of a crow's
quick black flight is a reflex
question(?). A realisation, though,
can be fast as a sparrowhawk
jigging and swerving between trees.
Gone. The wide-eyed mind printed
with the moment of its having been.

Sam Smith

Cold days are dangerous: foot-rags absorb bodily
moisture. As the men stand in ranks of ten to be
counted the lowest layers freeze to the ground.
Their staggering free has them barge into
other prisoners. Makes the guards nervous.

> Rats burrow among the graves. Even the guards
> don't like that, ask where are the dogs they
> shot at. The kitchen-fed cat, at the back of
> the guardhouse, chitters as he watches the slither-
> belly snake-tails, their thin pink tongues
> licking the bowls of freshly cracked eggshells.

Black branches and trunks of wind-blasted
trees have snow skeletons. Under washed-thin
shirts shiver-spasms jerk the skin about.
Men struggle to keep straight the decimal
rows, deny the magpie eater-of-eyes. But still
their heads are full of itch, their dripping
noses reeking of their own excretions.

Childhood has the practise death of pets. Hardest
now to notice is an absence, the past becoming what
the present wants it to be. Seeking and following
signs, men act on portents, only later discover
what they may have meant, their possible import.

> An officer drives impatiently into camp.
> The car door does not close. The radio,
> his journey's companion, has been left on.
> Across acres of compound the car talks to
> itself. But only male voices, in tones of
> discussion, can be heard, not the words.

The present can sentimentalise the past, recall
it with the slowness of sensuality, that brief
eternal moment of everyone's childhood – to be
celebrated or, if wronged, lamented ... In such
safe sure existences of the mind, loyalty is to lies:
those here who insist on the truth, if only to an own
private self, accuse that inner self of treachery.

Sam Smith

Crackle and flash of gunfire wakes them.
Then, at first light, artillery crumps
to the north. North makes no strategic
sense. The jets are theirs, rockets
a fizz, each explosion a momentary sun.

> In some men the repeated, and unfounded,
> rumours of release kill hope. In some to
> speak of freedom sustains its possibility,
> and nurtures hope. An amber under-glow to all
> green this day. One man gives in to death's
> seduction, hangs himself with a rope of rags.

When all of a man's charms have failed
– magpies, rainbows, touch wood & spit –
nothing worked, so where his luck? Politics
a confusion of simplicities, patriotism
a collective onanism: each man so tired
that the whole of his body is a-throb, wants
only to pupate into uninterrupted sleep.

Beak yellow as hawthorne leaves in autumn, a watched
blackbird runs across the guardhouse lawn. Stops.
Even here, a man can be the tankard of his own being;
but, always, on the edge of the small sensible calm
each man makes for himself, there are barbarians.

> A guard, his face a mask of intent, makes
> one man kneel, bend his head, shoots him
> in the hollow of the neck. On hut roofs
> wagtails bounce along, pause with a parkinsonian
> tremble. The prisoners do not know the man's
> offence, nor how he may have appeared offensive.

So the men look down: eye contact could
initiate the fever of slaughter. And most
men here have trembled on the edge of other
trenches. Old bubbled varnish freckles
odd planks and snail trails tinsel
the huts' sides. Beyond the fence, on yellow
grass tufts, spiders have spun grey candyfloss.

Sam Smith

Stones are moved from beside this hut
to beside that hut. Such work has
no reward. Those guards, who do not
like to behold squatting idleness
(who the keeper, who the kept?), watch.

> Ordered to At-The-Double!, bone thin, rags
> fluttering, certain that he is about to be
> shot, he runs with the unflappable dignity
> of an ostrich. Reaching a corner he keels over
> onto his back, stares, alive, gasping
> up at a world gone skyworm bright.

Old tape, on a curled-over notice, is
yellow and brittle. Glowing, just beyond
the green and glistening trees, part curved
over the grey mountain, incongrous and benign,
are a rainbow's colours, translucent and
ephemeral as wishes. Two tidy white doves walk
sideways to the apex of the hut's gable end.

All night a cow bellows. Milk fever, says
one man. Calf breeched, says another.
Cut off from the herd, stuck in a bog,
another. The men, detritus of other men's
ambitions, lie awake in disorderly rows.

> Most once-mounds have one
> almost vertical, wooden
> marker. Each stela is allowed
> one name, a few a set of
> initials. None can carry
> an incriminating date.

The living here are not brave men: the angry died
fighting. The men here seek only to survive. Those
driven by ideals and indignation will not: they
will not read the irritation in the old guard's mouth,
the anxiety in the younger's eyes. A weak man staggers.
Two guards, shouting, beat him down. A third
comes rushing between them to kick the body.

Sam Smith

A line of saw-edged cloud moves slowly through
the land space between trees and mountain. Between
trees and fence stand white cows, their wide breaths
and flat flanks steaming. Mist has laced the fence
with webs, cross-threads moored to razor tips and barbs.

> One de-horned steer rubs his shoulder
> against a corner post. The lattice
> of wire trembles a sparkle of drops.
> The guards have gone. The men,
> although curious, continue in
> the safety of their habits.

Drab military vehicles arrive, park in formation. Soldiers
move among the prisoners, try to shake hands, to embrace.
Two mud-streaked cars stop beside the guardhouse. Men
in civilian jackets are consulted. Two women reporters,
shoulder-hung with equipment, stand backs to the camp, talk
rapidly into microphones and cameras. One woman official
has round calves: her high heels go pinking along the road.

In green army caravans sour-faced nurses
strip/delouse the men. Cursing doctors
give injections. Each naked man is handed
white trainers and a blue tracksuit too large.
"They're ashamed of us," word goes out.

> Outside, soldiers walk with young men's
> pavement swagger. " ... ashamed of us."
> a doctor, hearing the prisoner's whisper,
> cries out, "No! No!" Printed notices
> have been stapled to hut sides
> – BIG MEALS WILL KILL YOU.

A bonfire has been made of their rags: a white sun
hangs in the speckled smoke. Coaches, agleam with wet
and windows, slide between huts. Soldiers, holding lists,
herd prisoners, hand them up the metal steps. Cameramen
walk backwards along the queues. Flat of hands
test the short bristles of the seats,
back and buttocks rock their softness.

Sam Smith

Each coach has to reverse into the compound
to turn. Each window has at least one face
waiting for the wire fence to pass. Beyond the so
few trees, ribboned off, is a sparkling minefield
of buttercups, daisies and brown plantain heads.

> Scattered over cratered ground (already
> overgrown) are the chalk-coloured
> rumps of serviced ewes; then stacks
> of black plastic bales – soft eggs
> pregnant with silage. Two magpies
> sit aslant a high wooden stile.

Among fields, flat and furrowed as the sea,
an island stand of trees has a scrapyard of cars,
mostly red, boots and bonnets open like so many
dark-coloured birds perished and petrified in
each their moment of alighting. The right-left
left-right swing of a level crossing's red lights
holds them, barrier reflectors like continuation dots …

In the coaches away large men from Army Intelligence
walk the rubber-floored aisles, sit themselves beside
prisoners; a ridged lake of glasshouse roofs; a sloping
field of slung-bellied ewes; light made liquid upon
a reservoir's surface; purple mountain receding.

> A kestrel perches hunched upon a road sign,
> another hovers over an embankment of
> yellow broom. Plump women with pursed mouths
> drive fast cars: in their side windows
> a pale day-moon's transparent reflection.
> In a side road a car sunk onto its flat tyres.

"There," a man prods a face-on photograph in a plastic
sheath, "That's one." Grey bales, broken apart, reveal
gold behind; a magpie climbs the roadside sky; low
brick walls separate pavement from bungalow garden;
slender stem of a young woman's waist rises
out of the bowl of her hips; gym-toned bodies
pose semi-naked, muscles about to burst the skin.

Sam Smith

Dry spaces have been left in the car park
neat as hospital beds newly made. Beyond
the buildings' backs a small town's everyday
hellos, horn beeps and waves. The soldiers
and policemen are rattled by the women's fussing,

> by their display of emotion, their breaking
> ranks to reclaim a remembered face, their
> crying out and fluttering around their
> emaciated man. The children look on mute:
> no-one has told them how to behave. Aware of
> the cameras, one adolescent will tell friends

later of her mother shouting and weeping, will say,
"I didn't know where to put my face."
The held men look sideways upon these familiar
strangers called family, at the cliffs and crevices
of their faces; and they marvel at having used
as foundations such soft stones – on which once
to build a life, now disbelieve the building.

In the blood-thick dark thoughts coagulate and
clot. Pressed to the bottom of night's trough,
gasping a wet panic, one arm reaches up, numb
finger and thumb cuts into the black fug with
a snick. Bedside lamp throws light up the wall.

> Phlegm, on a piece of rubbery string, coughs up
> and down the epiglotis. Yesterday
> he was shown photographs – left & right profile,
> full face on – of men he'd avoided looking at
> by men who will, today, still believe in justice.
> Lavatory flush refills, boiled kettle clicks off.

Sink-back spider, grown enormous on detritus, folds
its legs in through the overflow. On the kitchen radio
the religious self-blow their bugles: at this bleak hour
a trumpetting aimed at the isolated, the rootless,
the drifting; bibles in hotel rooms, beside hospital beds
– primed to explode into fractal minds. He switches
the radio off, and coughs – invocation for an atheist.

Sam Smith

Hands on the stairwell's metal rail he lets
the building's electrical hum enter him. Fridge
motors, heating pumps, radio and TV vibrations
are absorbed into the plaster and concrete.
The structure's internal iron becomes voice.

> He goes from room to room, switches on
> the TV, changes channels. Time here is
> out of joint. In nano-seconds he is moved
> to subjects new and places distant. He leaves
> the room. Turns on the radio. Another speaker,
> somewhere else. He leaves the room.

Down in the street a man and two women talk
together. The man makes the two women laugh.
A dog passes sniffing. A boy, delivering pamphlets,
goes down the stairs singing the same few words.
A letterbox clatters; and he starts again.
Graffiti opposite still says, 'Life is not as simple
as a slogan. This is a slogan.' He leaves the room.

In a household of ordinary secrets, where
cupboard doors are always closed, where life
is kept in quiet order, lest the greater chaos
intrude, his puddled night-sweats are born of
fears worse imagined. She moves to comfort him.

> Only in the lime-waiting pits does naked flesh
> meet naked flesh. Night's sour eye sees a cunt
> shape of a canoe, clitoris waiting to be paddled.
> His back turned, she creeps out of bed, sits on
> the lavatory, and weeps. Alone next day, bathroom
> door locked, expressionless he masturbates.

No pleasure to be had from this remedial sex,
no dark and proud delight in one single pearl
of semen. And, come evening, she seeks the soporific
of soaps – the televisual experience that is no
experience, a surface sensation that doesn't reach
the seat of memory. While he, sat in the kitchen,
speculates on the characters of wooden spoons.

Sam Smith

He watches a child of the rape
play with a push-toy. The mother
keeps coming back to the room,
makes unanswered smalltalk. He,
unmoving, watches the child.

> Where the empire of the kettle
> starts the day, acres of small
> square houses are set at angles
> to one another, Cul-de-sacs off
> Crescents, looping back to their
> beginnings, insular as the deaf.

The mother makes kissing noises as she sucks on
her thin roll-up. Ordinariness requires the repetition
of routines. Leaving, he declares that he will fall
only into the rhythms of a garden, undertake only
its replicated chores, hoeing and mowing. He will
not step onto the treadmill of work. The cold is
carried back indoors with him on his clothes.

Every working and domestic routine seems trivial,
timetables of no real consequence. They, who call
themselves his wife, his son, his daughter, his
parents, their friends, talk of a past they presume
he shares. He remembers their stories.

> A cosmopolitan city this, without the singular
> stamp of bigoted authority, moves about its
> business. Autobiographical philosophies not yet
> met others' realities, men walk here, though, who
> are aware of the mechanics of myth; but who still
> know themselves to be prisoners of their histories.

Pavements have known faces, with lives imagined;
turds that crust themselves over, seal in their
odour. On long legs a thin and dying cat, wanting
to be let in, totters against a blue door. Everyone
has left for work. The hall stinks of hair-spray
and fresh perfume. He watches a silver thread of air
being spun down the emptying plug. Again.

Sam Smith

To avoid the sudden quickness of boys,
the tedious slowness of men, eager bonhomie
of bores (self-congratulation of some survivors,
or lengthy bemusement – why them?) he side-
steps into this corner, dodges round the next.

> A cement-stippled house, windows once board, has
> cindered and black-glinting roof spars already
> darkened and dappled by trees growing over. Rooms'
> corners have drifts of dry leaves. In disrepair
> the walls look thin, cheap: a past/ a present
> that was/ is only fodder for a future.

The slipping-by presence of mice and old smoke's
wet tang makes him uneasy. He ducks out under
a broken lintel. In the next street he sees new
houses with, one day, ferns, even trees, growing
up inside: one window smashed and spindled
seeds will blow through, slot into floorboard
cracks, await the releasing moisture of rot.

Another psychotherapist looks on, with the cold/
cold eye of a comedian/assassin, waiting his/her
chance. He stands, walks from the room,
turns this corridor corner, the next. Leaving
the building he steps blindly into light.

> Stopped by a metal barricade he
> watches the traffic stop/flow – lorries,
> cars. More cars – men masked alone;
> four fat men turning inwards to
> laughing talk; a woman smiling
> forward, two children sat in back.

He turns this street corner, the next.
Thru'way noise becomes like sea on
a hidden beach. Deep in a canal cutting
green moss grows rounded out of red brick.
A new fern slowly uncurls its chameleon
tongue. He turns this corner, the next. Single
tree shadow gives a wall veins and arteries.

Sam Smith

Tail erect, the cat steps between
doorstep bottles, newly washed,
ever bigger bubbles spanning
their insides: part rainbows
been collected, left out to dry.

> On the ceiling a poster of primary-coloured
> fishes. "Poor diet," the masked dentist says
> as he steel-picks, scrapes and probes. Cotton
> wadding deforms the lip. A pump gurgles down
> between dried cheek and gum. Comes the insect
> whine of the wet drill, stone grind of the slow.

A uniformed girl, hugging tubes of beakers,
stumbles up the stairs. In the waiting room
crumpled magazines and thought-cancelling
radio drivel. Interrupted. News of the latest
barbarity comes via the latest technology.
Just inside the church door a statue of a saint,
a halo plate balanced on his head.

Night griffin sits asquat a tower. Stone
lion claws splinter into the thin roof.
Eagle wings unfold to steady its perch.
Raptor's beak points this way, that;
eyes will decide, on impulse, its meal.

> To escape dream's isolation he turns this
> corner, the next; passes chauffeur-gleamed
> cars. On a swept tennis court two men face
> each other with the aching smile-muscles of
> game players, their every action still saying
> the little boy's "Watch me! Watch me!"

He sits in a public lavatory to listen to
the gurgle of his insides. In a cafe he watches
a fat man sneak food into himself. Under
pavement tables sparrows boss each other. Pale
watercolours of mountain scenes are for sale. On
her morning break, cup cooling, a tired woman
looks down the previous day's share listings.

Sam Smith

Governments, no matter what their colour,
each with troublesome citizens,
are sympathetic to one another,
act always too late to smother
any monster they may have helped create.

> The bombing campaign, that they boast
> brought about his release, also killed
> his wife and three sons. A tarpaulin
> covers the shell of the house he now
> shares with two bombed-out families.
> Face masked he watches their children.

Space of his mind knows that somewhere else, now,
more huts are being built, new fences tightened.
A single leaf spins on a spider's single thread.
The young couple next door were taken, their rooms
now smoke-blackened. In passing a chorus of flies
rises from the sun-warmed brick. The doormat is
intact, although green with twin-leafed seedlings.

From his cafe seat he watches people queue at
a supermarket checkout, sees each as dulled,
in rags, shuffle each into the next empty
space. Not the kind of people who read novels:
life, therefore, always taking them by surprise.

> On canal towpaths, men and women, living within
> their quiet lives of cliche, pass by full of
> suspicion, each part of their life, bodily function
> and emotion, labelled and categorised; yet most
> know only that they are lost, do not fit; sad,
> lacklustre souls, unable to avoid the predictable.

With hatreds harboured in the anonymity
of this universal suburbia; these, the small town
singleminded (potential guards), own a caretaker's
murderous anger at an unappreciative
dirtying world. This spite is aimed especially
at the (disrespectful) young – their eyes aglitter
and hungry for every one of life's experiences.

Sam Smith

With a snail trail of semen on his thigh he delights
in the ordinary – letterbox snick and shush of
envelopes, quiet voices through open windows …
Yet he says to her, "What strange creatures we
monogamists are, giving our lives to each other."

> So delicately is this, his world, kept
> together, that it needs only the slightest
> miscalculation for the whole of any
> being to collapse. Puzzled, she thinks
> herself hurt by his words. And now …
> now there is a shouting family next door.

"My family," he says, "didn't talk of love. Not for
our parents, nor for our brothers and sisters. Only
of duties and resentments." Getting up, radio on,
he goes from room to room, pursued by pop music, its
repetitions finding folds in his mind. "Sentimentality,"
he too needs to be shouting, "is fundamentally a lie.
Religion and poetry are there only to teach us how to die."

The first notes pressed by the pianist bite
into lemon. So, wincing, he begins; searching
out, picking up, letting drop themes, like a dog
in a flat meadow hunting lost scents. Then, for
a long moment, flying lazily straight as a crow.

> Her talk is a defining and re-defining of
> friends, always reporting some of her own acts
> of kindness – her building up, superstitiously,
> a store of goodwill to herself. Some friendships
> she uses as fashion accessories – they look
> good on her. (This is how civilisation works?)

Birdsong after rain, the piano sings
itself awake again. Then, in a moment,
with the certainty of hatred, a hammered out
tune. Washed away with the hesitations of,
tentatively with, the fingertip touches of
love. One slow deep breath, salt-lick smooth.
Last note – a dark leaf dropped to ground.

Sam Smith

Simple laws can govern a life, but
life – this present pierced by the past
and held against the future – is
never simple: takes half a century
at least to get over the last big war.

> Pretty, a quirky smile, she has
> spent so long facing mirrors
> she thinks the image her.
> White paper package of garlic,
> broken open, has a striated
> agate interior, pungent odour.

On childhood's face the enigma of not
knowing can alternately intrigue and enrage
a survivor. Child told, this new knowledge,
held inside, walked about on the same legs
as an hour before, each re-detonation contained
behind everyday's mask and carried from plane
to plane, the familiar is made strange.

Crimes committed against the parents do not
justify the crimes of the children. Yet most,
ineptly evil, is simply the spill-over anger
of young men – coming to terms with this once-only
life, too many chances already missed, not dealt.

> People, around about the market, are as
> busy and gregarious as farmyard sparrows.
> The wind band, on its small podium,
> smells of spit dribbled and dripped
> from brass valves and woodwind ends,
> soaked into cuffs and spotting the floor.

On this to-be-momentous day – of manufactured
incident, food for future anecdote (to be as
contrived in the telling as the event's making),
other men still have to unload lorries, nurses empty
commodes, cows have to be milked, some killed.
Throughout a man atop an aluminium ladder, with red
bucket and squeegee, will be washing squares of sky.

Sam Smith

Flies crawl a moon's sea of frying pan fat. Mandibles,
of a tail-pulsing wasp, scrape the transparent stone
of glass. Bent forward he studies the bent forward
posture of a young mother, stooping to the baby
in the pram, a toddler holding on.

> A refugee, any refugee, must go blundering
> into settled lands. Steps knock thought
> upon thought into a rhythm, heels tap
> out a shape. Following an inward tread
> of ideas, he turns this corner, the
> next. Worlds open under his stride.

Speculating on transience and dis-
continuity: statistics may change, quality
of war remains constant – in types of muti-
lation, deformed births. Non-absolutes
are what matter, relevant positionings
in space/time/future. He halts at the
circular infinity of this planet's seas.

Night's white clouds creep up the hillsides.
Down below a bridge wall, this indigo dawn,
a duck – her flat bill wing-tucked – asleep
on a bed of bright green weed. A single tree
on one hilltop – a lollipop on a stick.

> Pauses made in any journey, a man will think,
> in the cessation-of-movement stillness, yes, here,
> this place, I could live this life. And his feet
> will go following made-memories' paths, glancing back
> over inscapes, nodding in pleased recognition:
> a birchwood's twin verticals of white & grey. Yes.

Here, within this forest, sun lasers down through
gap-lens in the canopy. Around water-shaped rocks,
below grub-laced leaves of alder, stream
bubble-foam gets mixed with cartwheeling
thistledown, revolving rotates in eddies.
In an open sky, excess of light, a waterfall's
tight silver thread slices back into the mountain.

Sam Smith

Comes a craving for the stillness of forests, to be
among elm's green tincture and moss-grown oaks,
honeysuckle nests of old dried leaves querying eye's
corners, ash's fruits glowing golden in an evening sun;
to lie by a glass-green river, under a bobbled alder.

> No antidote to beauty's bite – a venom that must
> connect mind/eyes to pinprick stars and wind
> sculpted form, a poison to render ears susceptible
> to the architecture of symphonies, a toxic that
> will be pleased only by the elegance of intellect.
> Victims die sighing over small satisfactions.

Promise of light has him step from the watched privacy
of the forest and into a clearing – made of storm-
shattered boughs, snapped saplings; and bordered by
the darker secrets of squat yews, red berries like
wax sweets like soft beads. Beside them laurel fruit
bruise green into purple. Dried brown docks imitate
the fox: a sat still fox mimics a dried brown dock.

On a redbrick station platform a youth sits
polishing a silver euphonium. At a cliff base
beyond a girl lies across promenade slabs,
baggy clothes masking her shape, hair golden,
an angel husked and fallen like a leaf to earth.

> Fellow travellers on a train, never to be seen
> again, forgotten at journey's end; but, for these
> travelling hours, he weaves his being to theirs,
> covertly learns their faces, questions their gestures.
> For himself, he wears an inward stare, so
> intense, that it must repel all advances.

Among these quaintly restored cottages was once
a time of iron wheels rolling over cobbles, granite
egg-ends that now bruise soft-soled shoes. Back then,
in clogs, only the walked neighbourhood was known;
and the iron-shod cruel passed swiftly through.
Now, along the tops of backyard walls, cats, with
singleminded delicacy, patrol their territories.

Sam Smith

Bottom-sided gulls, pink feet tucked flat,
wheel up over the cliff's horizon with
a skateboarder's gravity-bound certainty.
Jackdaws, wings folded back, go skidding
down the wind, aslant the cliff's red face.

> Moored yachts, advertising their owner's
> wealth, dip and nod like so many spring
> tailed terns afloat. A big ship's ropes
> are cast off, snip-snip of a spider's web
> setting it adrift. Under way its wake becomes
> a white snail trail on the blue on blue sea.

Intent on being somewhere else on a map,
areas of travel – airports, stations,
docks – are populated by anxious faces.
Yet each is passive, contained each
within its tube of time, locked onto
a dotted line on each its map, or frowning
at stylised geometric rail configurations.

Lizard-brown skin oiled, here are slack-breasted
old men and women; no material cleverly cut
to disguise the short fat legs and hanging guts,
the bellies balanced by bums. The young are
thin, light-footed, have summer sun-glinting hair.

> The future has happened: he is old now. With
> the stop/start spasms of a stalking heron, he
> walks his body of scars among wet bellemite
> bullets from prehistory; there a finger-grooved
> ammonite half-shell – still curled upon itself;
> there an ovoid pebble whiter than an egg.

Pink rounded brick, glass frosted green at its once edges;
on a grey pebble a rash of hollow-eyed barnacles: tideline
of reed straws and brittle brown bladderwrack has a crow's
feather two shades of black, a rubber teat, ends of sawn
wood, blue toothbrush, bleached boards (nail stained),
frayed nylon rope, crisp sponges, polystyrene eggsac clusters,
aerosol caps, plastic trays (broken), a glass bottle intact.

Sam Smith

Attuned to time's forgetfulness he follows
the jagged flight of a single white
butterfly in a straight course out over
a light-shifting lake. At water's edge
a fallen pine rests on thin alligator legs.

> Open heathland has him panting like a hot day dog that
> wants only shade in which to lay and stretch his belly.
> Among rocks and green bracken is coiled a sinuous
> collection of dark diamonds. Has he come thus far
> to put his hand in there? Both enlivening danger
> and definition-by-death attracts.

Beyond the beach, in an offshore mist,
is the sun's white disc and drone of a motorboat.
Thin black flies crawl the soft hump of dried-out
tideline – brittle black bladderwrack, reed straws,
salt-bleached winkle shells, green semi-melted plastic,
a red & rusted cartridge case … One brown & purple
butterfly dips along the slow wavelength.

A brown mist of feathery grassheads whispers
around his ankles. Tits perch sideways to peck
out black mites from crackling barley ears.
From the hollow underside of laid-over dried
stalks comes the glass thin singing of mice.

> First sign of this ruin is a garden rose
> gone wild. Last act of a sparrow hit
> by a car is to tuck its beak under its
> wing. Across parched fields, boundaried
> by ditches, are roofs and walls, still
> standing, of some of the village houses.

Wearing green plastic leggings and aprons
three men, in a sloping concrete yard, stoop
to cut up a freshly killed fresian. In cages
behind them hounds bark and snarl. Black &
white skin has been peeled back. Slicing into
the red/pink flesh the men – in deep voices
– explain their world to one another.

Sam Smith

In the chill of a clear summer morn, sat
outside with a cup of coffee, low cloud
shaping the hills, he reads the paper.
Grey webs go funnelling into green hedges.
A steam train goes sawing up a valley.

> Butterflies, red & black, alight on
> bruised apples. Conjoined slabs of giant
> charolais change marbled tone as each
> moves. Black crows, in pairs, walk and
> waddle from one khaki pile to the next, leave
> a flattened fibrous spread of beak-pocked dung.

Rainwashed mountain sheep have had their fleece
crimped. From breathless mountain crags can be
seen a downward swoop of shale scree, blue eye
of a corrie, squared-off fields; and there, possibly,
a screen of conifers. Towers? Hut roofs? Past events lie
just under the dust of forgetfulness. When will time
overtake these/those years, erode their significance?

Rhythm of walking in the rustle/rustle of
his anorak hood, slush and mud underfoot;
attuned to time's forgetfulness in this
dusk and damp of winter; he is startled
by the crickle-crackle of unshed seeds.

> In among trunk bones of beech, old scars
> flat like cement on the bark, last year's
> nut husks are four-petalled wooden flowers.
> Pond bottom rot cooks methane up through
> bright weed, makes a melt-hole. Sharp snow
> prints show deer have been here to drink.

Below the split clothing of orchard bark the green
sinewed roots of mistletoe grip into the pith. Yeasty
squashed apple smell rises vinegary sweet as vomit.
From four trees behind comes the clucking of field-
fares, who, feeling safe, feast on the broken open
apples. Ahead an olive-backed sparrowhawk
goes pulsing low along the darkening road.

Sam Smith

A three-dimensional mesh of
threaded membranes, the whole fungus
is thickest at its subterranean
base, on the surface manifests
itself in a phallic obtusence.

> At birth a baby's first breath is when
> its lungs are released from womb-sac
> compression; death a final exhalation.
> The further from the reality of death
> the more he fears it: amidst it daily
> he fatalistically awaited his turn.

Now he walks in charcoal night, hedge flowers
chalked in moonlight, car beams drawing moving
shadows on moving walls of fog. Drops depend from
honeysuckle tendrils, glass-point rounded leaves.
A slug rears up off the road to sense the breeze,
detect the nearest vegetation. Come morning these
held droplets will have become a cleansing frost.

Startled by the red inside of a magpie's
black beak, ghost bray of a train taunting
distance, hawk cry measuring sky, he has
no faith to take refuge in, no certainty
of unknowns, no assuredness of guessed-ats.

> In this world grown too conscious of mirrors
> the more the young seek an identity the less
> meaning it has. His life in the camps is,
> to them, not so much unthinkable as not yet
> thought about. He says to none of them,
> "We are not wise, we who simply survived."

At sight of its returning mate – grey cape upon
an orange angular span – the nesting kestrel
chitters from its pasture oak. Walk and waddle,
below, of magpie and carrion crow are identical to
the ponderous self-important dawdle of any farmer
over his own fields. The farmer's offended shout
carries always the hard edge of the reactionary.

Sam Smith

Bee colonies infest cracks in trackside clay. Stone-
backed partridges move through a coat of green blades
laid over. Cottongrass, spiking a marsh, makes
a tired army of tattered plumes. Where naked rock
starts, coiling cloud peoples itself with legend.

> He walks head down, sky's stones facing his face.
> Rarely, up close, is a mountain a single peak.
> The mind looks down on, is locked down by a jig
> saw of routines and duties – work and back, family
> chores; and collapse to bed. Lives gloved together,
> fields interlocking, life making a kind of order.

A line of trees screens a road from houses,
houses from a road. In a world become again
tabloid simple, slaughter justifying slaughter
justifying slaughter, he knows that somewhere,
way way out of sight, waves are arranging
themselves to come always in straight lines
to whichever shore he will be standing on.

Sam Smith

Mistlethrush drives the foraging crow from
its bough-forked nest. An old widow walks
below, balancing her collection, of clicks
and aches, on each paining foot. The apple
tree in bloom, the mistletoe is unseen.

> Left alone children get locked behind
> tight faces, make desperate repair to
> things gone secretly wrong – a VCR,
> a cooker, a pen, a brother's toy ...
> Minded out, they meet another
> choirmaster child molester.

Old men sit and watch; and long to be again
as lightfooted as the young; as boys, released
from cars, who go bounding over peat-sprung
moors; and who instantly get busy doing what is
important to boys – running, seeing, being seen.
The girls pass quietly on elf tip-toe, go wade in
the shade, minnows nibbling at their white toes.

In doubt of life's worth he watches the small
being busy at what they do – wasps building
cities of paper, swallows flying low over
stubble, rooks marking out an autumn sky –
is amazed anew at their complexity of purpose ...

> To simply be, he holds the quietude of drizzle
> folding itself up a combe; smiles at a plough's
> lace sail of gulls, at half a rainbow plugged
> into a hill. Or, reversing cause and effect,
> he lets himself see stone erode rain,
> a pond's reflection attract sun's disc ...

... beholding this microbe miracle of inter-dependent
life, and how it all, every tiny movement, adds up,
throughout space and time, into a part of him
and him a part of it – the mutable constancy of
mountains, constrained freedom of birds, latency
of fungus, eye's breadth of oceans, numinosity of
night's firmament, reassurances of self's in/significance.

Sam Smith

Up here crag-perching ravens.
In combes below buzzards gliding.
Each species confined to its level,
its habitat, migratory routes, patterns
of existence. Where then freedom?

> The planet's crust curves out
> from under his feet in Mountain
> King visions. Down there maggot
> lozenge sheep crawl over a domed
> green hill, the river at its side
> a silver apostrophe/admonition.

Mammals too, moles and voles, each are caged
by their territory, diet and reproductive cycle.
A man's limits are also inside his being,
habits and attitudes trapping him in roles
and behaviours, no matter where he migrates;
and the species is bound, every so often,
to include a rogue who will turn on his own.

Small-leafed plants creep out of
old geological cracks and the slight
susurrus of a raven's open-beaked
flight gets confused with the white wisp
pouring up over broken rocks of mist.

> From among this damping cloud comes the calf
> call of another raven. Up here too a haunting
> of gulls, which fly one by one along cliff edges,
> appear as a coalescing of water droplets; or,
> unseen, with echo overlaying echo, they encourage
> their canyon tribe to sadness with sad cries.

From this summit's eroding scree, see – through
a momentary thinning of cloud – village roofs
tucked away on a river's bend; a city's dots
fingering up into hills from a wavering coast;
know that the land is in control of all these
small dwellings; that, in a transitory world
all is in transit. Before cloud encloses again.

Other Books by Sam Smith

NOVELS:

Crime
Sister Blister (also published as *The Wall*).
Marks (also published as *Hit and Run*).
Porlock Counterpoint.
Sick Ape: an everyday tale of terrorist folk.
Marraton (also published as *Failures of Love*).
The Company Chronicles.

Mainstream
The Paths of Error trilogy: *Undeclared War,*
                           Constant Change,
                           and *As Recorded.*

2 Bridgwater Days.
Eviction from Quarry Cottages.
The Care Vortex.
Something's Wrong.
Everyday Objects Repurposed as Art.
Trees.
The Seventh Man?

Sci-Fi
The End of Science Fiction.
John John.
We Need Madmen.
Once Were Windows Once Were Doors.
An SF quintet comprising of: *Balant,*
                             Happiness,
                             You Human: the Leander Chronicle,
                             Not Now: Death, Dreams, and Reasons for Living,
                             and *The unMaking of Heaven (Eternals).*

Sam Smith

Historical Fiction
The Secret Report of Friar Otto
The Friendship of Dagda and Tinker Howth

Non-fiction
Vera & Eddy's War
Sam Smith's prose pieces
Anti

POETRY COLLECTIONS

To Be Like John Clare, University of Salzburg Press.
Skin&Bones, Odyssey Poets.
Dialogues, Silver Gull Publishing.
John the Explorer, Gecko Press.
pieces, K.T.Publications.
Rooms, Oasis Books.
apostrophe combe, boho press.
Problems & Polemics, boho press.
Rooms & Dialogues, boho press.
Canoe, erbacce press.
An Atheist's Alphabetical Approach to Death, erbacce press.
A New Acmeism, erbacce-press.
Local Colour, Indigo Dreams.
Speculations and Changes, KFS.
Problems and Polemics, Wordcatcher.
Rooms, Wordcatcher.
In the hand, Trivium.
Mirror Mirror, erbacce.